The
POWER OF
WORDS

Rev J Martin

DEDICATION

I dedicate this book to my mother who always believed
that I would do great things with my life.

CONTENTS

ACKNOWLEDGMENTS

I would like to thank everyone that made this book possible. To all that support me and continue to support me, this includes YOU.

1 POWER IN WORDS

Most people do not understand how powerful their words are. Words have the power to start wars, or end relationships. They have the power to build trust, loyalty, and love. Where you are, in your life right now, has a lot to do with what you have been saying about yourself.

Your words are like seeds; seeds can turn into something real. Whether or not you realize it, you are continually building your future with the words you speak. For example, there is no point applying, because I will never get the position. You have closed that door permanently in your future.

When saying things like, I'm so lucky to have my health, I'm so grateful to have a job, I will fulfill my dreams, I'm coming out of debt, you are not just being positive; you are being thankful and predicting good things for your future.

We will find that our life always moves toward our words. Too many people predict the opposite of what they want. I get no luck. I will never lose weight. There is always something to bring you down.

People who say these things don't realize it, but they are laying the wrong foundations; they are prophesying defeat and then wondering why they are unhappy with their lives. They are welcoming bad luck, giving them an excuse to eat more, expecting to lose their jobs.

Proverbs 18:21
The tongue has the power of life and death, and those who love it will eat its fruit.

You are planting the seeds for your future when you talk. At some point, you will eat that fruit. My challenge is to make sure you are planting your favorite fruit. If you love Blueberries, plant Blueberry seeds. If you want Blueberries, you wouldn't set apple seeds or pear seeds.

You can't expect to speak negative all the time and live a positive, healthy life. You can't talk defeat and experience victory. You can't talk about everything going wrong and expect everything to go right. If you have poor words, then you will have a poor life.

If your life is not going as expected, then plant some new seeds. Instead of speaking lack, speak abundance. God didn't make one piece of grass; he made millions, not one drop of water, but an entire ocean.

2 RIGHT SEEDS

God delivers me everything I need; good things will come into my path. I provide an excellent service in the world and will never be without. I will live like Jesus, putting others before myself.

These are the right seeds. If you sow these seeds, eventually, you will eat the fruit of these words. Gods favor. Abundance. Greater understanding.

Instead of saying I will never shake off this sickness, say, this illness didn't come to stay; it came to pass. I'm getting better and better every day. My future is blessed with good health. Sow seeds of health, increase, and abundance. No more, I will never get better. I will never fulfill my dreams. 'I will never' has to come out of your vocabulary.

Instead of speaking sickness, talk health. I hear people talk for years about their aches and pains, and then they wonder why they are full of aches and pains.

They go to the doctor and ask for something to numb the pain, but that is like mopping up the water from a leaking bucket, instead of plugging the hole.

If they changed their words and asked the doctor what is causing the aches and pains, a good doctor would say, lack of exercise leads to the weakness and breakdown of muscles. Lack of water in your diet leads to stiffness and pain.

Remember, there is power in your words. I have the favor of God; only blessings are in my future. I will meet the people and opportunities to catapult me towards the life of my dreams. If you keep talking like this, you will reap a harvest of good things.

James 3:10

Out of the same mouth come praise and cursing. My brothers and sisters, this should not be.

Many people don't realize it, but with their words, they are cursing their future. When you speak in the negative about your future, then you have just cursed your life. I'll never get that new job; I'll never be able to afford to buy a new house. I'll never be healthy. You might not realize it, but when you speak this way, you are cursing your future.

Often, the enemy does not stop us; it is ourselves. Pay attention to what you are saying daily. Are you blessing your life or are you cursing it??

3 UNIVERSITY FRIEND

Gaz, a friend at university, would always speak negatively about his future. He was very talented, he played several instruments, was a very gifted actor, and he was a superb DJ, but he would invariably say, people where I come from get no breaks.

Ten years later, I met him. When I asked how things were going, his response, as I told you years ago, people where I come from get no breaks. Ten years later he was still saying it; he had said it so often that it became a self-fulfilling prophecy.

Don't speak defeat about your future, like my friend did. Let your attitude be: God is nurturing my talents, helping them grow. Opportunities come into my path, with the confidence and courage to grab them with both hands. I will live a successful, rewarding, and faithful life.

Stop going around cursing your future and the

future of others, and start blessing your life and the lives of others. Prophesy great things.

John, another friend at university, was the opposite. He wasn't that talented, but he had great faith and persistence. John believed that, with the grace of God, he would achieve great things. For many years, John just worked away on his dreams. Most of his friends thought he was crazy, but what they thought of him didn't matter. John knew what he wanted and never stopped going for it.

I respected him most for his persistence; if something didn't work, he would just change his approach. He always spoke of victory, never defeat. He had always loved music and had spent many years as an engineer. He also always had a burning passion for freestyle dance.

One day, he shocked everyone when he did a music video on YouTube that got played over 100,000 times. A top record label in London approached him, asking him to produce videos for them.

From today, you need to stop criticizing yourself, like my first friend did, focusing on what you don't want to happen and letting those thoughts flow into your words. I'm too ugly, too fat, and too slow. I get no breaks; there is always something to hold me back.

Instead, bless your life; speaking victory, even when defeat stares you in the face, knowing your destiny is full of great things. When you talk of success, then you will look at setbacks as learning experiences set in your path by God to develop your character.

4 THOUGHTS TO REALITY

This local farmer was very concerned about having a heart attack. His grandfather and a couple of his uncles had one around his age, which slowed them down, meaning, they could no longer work on their farms.

He started to say how he would have to slow down. He was only in his early 50s and was a bully of a man. In the summer months, working 18-hour days was normal for him.

He was already getting his son to do most of the work; he was convinced that his heart would fail. I watched as this healthy man with the energy of a man half his age, talked himself into a homebound state, being out of breath, even walking up stairs.

It is good to use common sense and not push yourself to the limit, but if you go around speaking about it, like this farmer, making plans for it, most likely you will not be disappointed. You are preparing for its arrival.

He was letting his negative thoughts flow into this words. I told him to stop saying he would have a heart attack. Instead, announce that he would live the rest of his life in good health. He would have the energy and passion for working on his farm well into his later years. Prophesy health. Prophesy a long productive life. Your words will become your reality.

Within a few months, he was back on the farm, back to full strength. To this day, I still see him putting up fences and cultivating his land.

5 WORDS OF YOUR MOUTH

Proverbs 6:2

You have been trapped by what you said, ensnared by the words of your mouth.

Ensnared means to be trapped, we can be trapped by the words of our mouths. We all think negative thoughts. The problem arises when we speak them. When we speak negatively about what we can achieve and ourselves, we have lost the battle in our minds.

Your words can lead your life in a particular direction. If you say, I will never get the promotion, then you blocked your own path. If you say, I will never get back into shape; you will always be overweight and have problems with your health.

When you speak negatively about yourself, you stop God's favor for your life. You were put here to evolve, to grow, and to expand. Don't set limits for who you are. Your words may have snared you in the past, but from today, you will be free from that trap. The shackles are broken.

You need to do your part and speak victory over your life. Take 'I can't, I will never, I couldn't', out of your vocabulary, replacing them with, I can do all things through God. I will face my fears, knowing God is by my side. Speak words of abundance, faith, health, love, and happiness. Stop using your words to describe the situation; learn to use your words to change the situation.

Matthew 6.31-33

So do not worry, saying, 'What shall we eat?' or 'What shall we drink?' or 'What shall we wear?' For the pagans run after all these things, and your heavenly Father knows you need them. But seek first his kingdom and his righteousness, and all these things will be given to you, as well.

As it says in Matthew 6, do not worry, speaking in the negative. Seek first his kingdom and all will be delivered to you. Too many of us concentrate on the negative, taking our minds off God, thinking we know best, letting what we fear hinder his favor.

Jesus was saying, you may feel worried, but do not give life to the thoughts of worry by verbalizing them. Don't get trapped by your words. Don't let your words put limits on your life. Let your words come into line with what God wants for you, success, love& happiness.

6 ESSENTIAL RENOVATIONS

My local church needed essential renovations to include proper wheelchair access and a new roof; it was something that had to be done. We got quotes, the best of which was $1,750,000. We had seen a decrease of the weekly collection since the recession, so to raise that kind of money in a small community would take a lot of work.

I could see no way we would raise the amount needed, but even though those thoughts were racing through my mind, I kept my mouth closed. I let no one else see or hear the worry I had within. I knew, for the project to go ahead, I needed to speak words of we can, we must, we could.

Its one thing to think something is impossible, but don't give life to the thoughts through your words.

When you do, they take on a whole new meaning, and they affect every ear that hears them.

You might think the pain in your leg will never go away. You might believe you will never get the planning permission to build a new house, never get the loan to pay for a new car. Those thoughts will naturally flow through your mind, like clouds across the sky; the problem arises when you give them life, by speaking them.

At our weekly meeting, everyone turned to me. They were all very discouraged and simply could not see a way, as on paper, it seemed impossible. I told them, currently, I see no way, but I know God has a way. God has not put this obstacle in our path, without giving us the means to overcome it. We need to think, speak, and act as if the funds are already coming in. It may seem impossible on paper, but with God, all things are possible.

I knew better than to curse my future, to ensnare others with words of defeat. I knew, if I encouraged abundance, favor, and good breaks, then we would move towards it.

When your back is up against the wall, and you cannot see a way, it's easy to vent your frustration, tell others how you've had the pain for months and months, how your son is nothing but trouble, how the people at work don't treat you right. When you always talk about the problems you face, not only will it frustrate you, stress and depress you, but you water that weed and give it more life; you are nurturing it, letting it become bigger.

Learn to turn it around. Don't talk about the problem; speak about the solution. Instead of saying I have this big challenge, say, I serve a big God. No problem is too big for him. If he put this before me, then he will give me the strength to overcome it.

Instead of complaining about not getting the new job, looking at it as another disappointment; know, when God closes a door, it means he has something better lined up for you.

When your friends say, I heard your neighbor did you wrong, say, yes, but I'm not worried. God is their judge, not me. He has promised me great things. I will not allow their negativity to take me down. I will realign my life with those who want good for me, those who want to take me to new levels, and I will not get caught up in the past.

Two-Face
There are always two voices battling in our minds for attention, the voice of faith and the voice of fear. You will hear a voice, like I did; its too much money, this community is small, and the recession has hit hard; there is simply no way. You will be tempted to worry, be stressed, and have sleepless nights. But if you quieten your mind, you will hear another voice, the voice of faith, telling you that God has a way. Favor is coming; healing is coming.

The voice of fear will list all the reasons you should

stay in the same job, the same bad relationship. The voice of faith will tell you all the reasons you are the perfect person for the job, there are better relationships in your future, and that God is by your side every step of the way. Your best days are still in front of you.

Life Lesson – You get to choose which voice comes to life. The way you do this is through the words you speak. When you verbalize a thought, you are giving it the right to come to pass. If you go around, saying the problem is too big, I'll never get well, you agree with the wrong voice. Get into agreement with God. The other voice may seem louder, but you can override it. You can take away all of its power by choosing the voice of faith.

Maybe you have to attend an important meeting. One voice will tell you that it will not go smoothly; you have wasted your time. The other people will not like what you have to say. Another voice will say, God is by your side, you are intelligent, you are confident, and what you have to say is exactly what they want to hear.

If you get up that morning and tell your partner, the meeting will not go well, they will not like me, or what I have to say, there is no point even going, your words are trapping you in fear.

How often do our words trap us? We say things, like I'm not intelligent, they won't like me, I'm too old to do that, and heart problems run in my family. We all do it occasionally; the problem arises when those words start to shape our destiny.

Stand up strong and say, I will not give life to any thoughts that don't help me become a better person than I am today. I will not speak sickness, lack, defeat, or fear. Instead, I will choose the voice of faith; it says that I am strong, healthy, and victorious in every endeavor.

A young man came to me, one day, with an idea to set up a donation page online. He got the idea from Breaking Bad, an American TV show. He continued to tell me that by getting our message out with social media, people with any connection to the area from all over the world could donate.

We set up the page and raised the funds within eight weeks.

7 DAVID'S APPROACH

When David faced Goliath, all the odds were against him. If he had verbalized his negative thoughts, they would have kept him from his destiny. Even though he was anointed to be king, his negative words would have kept him trapped on his father's farm.

He could have easily gone around saying, I know I have to face Goliath, but look at him. He's twice my size; he's got more experience, and more equipment. I don't see how this will ever work out.

Negative words can hold you back from fulfilling God's plan for your life. Don't fall into that trap; stop talking defeat, and stop talking about why it will not happen. You can pray in faith, ask God to turn it around, for him to do the impossible, but after that prayer, you talk about your sickness with family and friends; you still worry about your child, worrying whether they will ever straighten up. Those words have just canceled out that prayer

Turn Around Debt

A young man came to me recently; he had massive debt and simply could not see a way out. He was very distressed; all he would do was complain about his lack of money. I told him that his words were trapping him in poverty. He needed to stop those words in their tracks. I told him to say, Lord, you have done it for me in the past; I know you will do it for me in the future.

I asked him, is there anything you can do to earn more money? He told me they cut overtime at work. What about another job, I suggested. Many people are telling me that, but my job is easy. I can do as I please. A new job will mean I have to change.

So I asked him, do you want to be in this situation a year from now? He quickly answered, NO. Well, I continued, you will need to change your life. You must meet God halfway.

Don't let your words trap you; negative talk brings negative results. When you speak words of faith, victory, that's what, allows God to do the impossible. Say things, like God will nurture my talents and lead me to a job I love. I welcome God to work through me, to lighten up the world.

When David stood in front of Goliath, he looked him in the eyes and said, you come with a sword and a shield, but I come to you in the name of the Lord. This day, I will defeat you and feed your head to the birds of the air.

Notice, he was prophesying victory. He might have felt fear, but he spoke faith. I'm sure, as David walked out toward Goliath, he was saying, God, give me the strength and skill to beat Goliath. God's armor is all the help I need. David then picked up a rock, put it in a slingshot, fired, and that rock brought Goliath tumbling down.

When you face challenges in life, they can sometimes seem like giants; you have to do as David and say to that sickness, you are no longer welcome. I will defeat you.

A child might have been a problem for a long time, but know that it is only temporary. One day, it will turn around. Keep strong in your faith; knowing your child will follow your example. Always speak victory and success over your life.

8 SAVING A LIFE

I recently read a moving story about a young man, called Jacob. Jacob had enrolled in a music theory class at a beautiful California Community College in the small, sleepy town of Moorpark. He stood a little over 6 feet tall, was a reticent student, and didn't seem to fit in with others.

Jacob hardly ever attended class, but his music teacher took a liking to him, as he always looked like he had the weight of the world on his shoulders.

As weeks progressed and tests were given, Jacob did not do well. The homework he handed in was getting steadily worse. He never participated in the class discussion or offered to answer questions.

Finally, the end of the year exam arrived. When Jacob finished, he looked worn out and defeated. The teacher collected the papers and told the class the final grades would be given out on Tuesday morning at 9:00 a.m.

The teacher had a feeling the grade she would give him would be a turning point in his life. Tuesday came, and all students came and went, but no Jacob, then as the teacher was leaving, Jacob turned up.

He apologized for being late and asked could he please have his final exam and grade. His teacher could clearly see he looked terrible. His eyes were sunk with dark, black circles under them, and the hollows of his cheeks were drawn. His skin was pale, and his hair matted. He was wearing the same clothes he had worn for the last week.

Before the teacher could say a word, Jacob spoke to her, "I know that I am getting a bad grade. I realize that I have not been participating in class. I am lazy, selfish, stupid, and an ugly no-good-for-nothing person. I don't know why I even came today; I'm unhelpable, unlovable. I am a hopeless case with absolutely no future."

She could not believe her ears. When he had finished, she faced him, looked directly into his morose eyes and said, "Jacob, your final grade is an A." His reaction was one of total and complete surprise. "You are giving me an A? Me? Why would you give me an A when I did such a poor job in class, on my assignments, and in my final exam? Why would you do that?"

Her answer to Jacob was this. "Yes, you appear to be a D student, but you're an A person. You just need to apply yourself. I believe in you, now, and I will always believe in you. I want you to know that if you ever need help, I will always be here for you. Always, remember that. Believe in yourself. You are a beautiful person, and I want you to know that I love you."

At 10:00 p.m. that night when she was at home, her phone rang. It was the priest from Jacob's church, thanking her for saving his life. He told her that Jacob's older brother had always teased and bullied him, as he was jealous of his good looks and 6-foot frame. His parents were always away on business; meaning, Jacob's brother was his primary role model.

The day Jacob went to collect his final grade, he had left a note on his bed. It read: "I am sorry that I could not be the kind of son and brother you wanted me to be. All I ever wanted was to be loved. I am sorry for being unlovable. I will go now...you will find me in the closet. I am sorry for any inconvenience I have caused."

Jacob had written the note before his meeting with his teacher. His plan was to see his teacher one last time before taking his life, as she always made time for him. When she gave him an A and told him she loved and believed in him, that she would always be there, something changed within him.

Those few words of encouragement gave him hope. He felt positive for the first time in his life. He felt so good; he took a long walk in the surrounding hills, replaying the words in his head. Someone in his life had told him they loved him and would always be there for him. He forgot all about his plan to do away with himself.

Meanwhile, his brother found the note, went to the closet in Jacob's room, where they found a rope hanging from the rafters.

Give Other's A Word Of Hope

Your words have the power not only to change your life, but they can dramatically alter the lives of others. Know what you are saying. Teasing someone can seem funny, but be careful not to overstep the mark, as you never know what is going on in someone else's mind.

Remember your power when you speak, for you have more influence than you think. Your words may be the encouragement someone desperately needs. Take the time each day to acknowledge those you meet, and spend time with those who need it. You may be surprised by the difference you can make in someone's life.

9 NEW DECREE

Psalms 2:7
I will proclaim the Lord's decree:

A decree was written down, an official document. We should harness the power of our words, by writing our own decree. Write down your goals, what you would like to happen in your life. Any area you would like to see improved, write it down like it is already done.

Then, every day, declare that decree. Read it over a couple of times out loud. It's not enough to just think it. There is great power in our words.

When we say, hear, and feel a statement, it makes a profound imprint on us.

You can personalize your decree, but some things that should be on it are:

I am healthy.
I am talented.
I am confident.
I work in a job I love.
I am at peace, as I know God directs my life.

Speak words like this each day, and after a short time, those seeds will grow. They will not just change your outlook, but you will grow into them.

Your words have immense power; your words create your reality. Your words have the energy to shape your life. People who regularly talk sickness are rarely healthy, and those that talk defeat, are never victorious.

You are setting the seeds for your future with the words you speak. Over time, your decree will grow to be part of your daily vocabulary. Before long, it will be normal for you to say things like, I'm talented, I'm confident, and God directs my life.

Instead of being trapped by your words, you will be propelled by your words.

James 3:2
Indeed, we all make many mistakes. For if we could control our tongues, we would be perfect and could also control ourselves in every other way.

Your life is simply a reflection of the words you speak daily. Do you see abundance, blessings, and new growth?

If not, be conscious of the words you speak. When you get your words going in the right direction, your life will follow.

If you expect good breaks and speak words of love and understanding over your life, and the lives of others, you will see significant changes; you will be healthier, happier, and have more energy. You will overcome every obstacle that stands in your way.

You will become everything God has created you to be.

Job 22:28
You will also decree a thing, and it will be established for you; And light will shine on your ways.

Rev J Martin

ABOUT THE AUTHOR

I live on the northwest coast of Ireland. I use this medium to share my true voice. I wish to enlighten others and help them to see that God wants the very best for them. We often make it hard for him to enter our lives as we focus on the dark clouds rather than the silver lining.

In this growing digital frontier, I just want to shed a little light out into the world to light up people's lives, in the hope that they to will help inspire others, which will slowly but surely change the world, even in a small way.

Made in the USA
Columbia, SC
17 March 2018